Inspirational Journal Notebook

You Are Stronger Than You Think

DREAM BIG

NEVER QUIT ♡

Prove Them Wrong

THINK POSITIVE

NAME: _____

Thanks for being here today — You rock! ♡ —Sue

suewoodard

think positive

"Optimism is the most important human trait, because it allows us to evolve our ideas, to improve our situation, and to hope for a better tomorrow." ~ Seth Godin

NEVER EVER GIVE UP

think positive

"The best way to gain self-confidence is to do what you are afraid to do." – Unknown

MAKE IT HAPPEN

think positive

"Happiness often sneaks in through a door you didn't know you left open." – John Barrymore

BELIEVE YOU CAN

think positive

"When we are no longer able to change a situation, we are challenged to change ourselves." – Viktor Frankl

BELIEVE IN YOURSELF

think positive

"If you can change your mind, you can change your life." – William James

TAKE ACTION!

think positive

"When the world pushes you to your knees, you're in the perfect position to pray." – Rumi

NEVER EVER GIVE UP

think positive

"The next time you feel slightly uncomfortable with the pressure in your life, remember no pressure, no diamonds. Pressure is a part of success." – Eric Thomas

MAKE IT HAPPEN

think positive

"You must make a decision that you are going to move on. It wont happen automatically. You will have to rise up and say, 'I don't care how hard this is, I don't care how disappointed I am, I'm not going to let this get the best of me. I'm moving on with my life." – Joel Osteen

BELIEVE YOU CAN

think positive

"Be soft. Do not let the world make you hard. Do not let pain make you hate. Do not let the bitterness steal your sweetness. Take pride that even though the rest of the world may disagree, you still believe it to be a beautiful place." – Kurt Vonnegut

BELIEVE IN YOURSELF

think positive

"Happiness, like unhappiness, is a proactive choice." – Stephen Covey

TAKE ACTION!

think positive

"Success is falling nine times and getting up ten." – Jon Bon Jovi

NEVER EVER GIVE UP

think positive

"All things are difficult before they are easy." – Thomas Fuller

MAKE IT HAPPEN

think positive

"You are never too old to set another goal or dream a new dream." – C.S Lewis

BELIEVE YOU CAN

think positive

"The difference in winning and losing is most often...not quitting." – Walt Disney

BELIEVE IN YOURSELF

think positive

"When I do good, I feel good. When I do bad, I feel bad. That's my religion." – Abraham Lincoln

TAKE ACTION!

think positive

"Whatever you want to do, do it now. There are only so many tomorrows." – Michael Landon

NEVER EVER GIVE UP

think positive

"There is little difference in people, but that little difference makes a big difference. The little difference is attitude. The big difference is whether it is positive or negative." – W. Clement Stone

MAKE IT HAPPEN

think positive

"If someone tells you, "You can't" they really mean, "I can't." – Sean Stephenson

BELIEVE YOU CAN

think positive

"The difference between stumbling blocks and stepping stones is how you use them." – Unknown

BELIEVE IN YOURSELF

think positive

"We are responsible for what we are, and whatever we wish ourselves to be, we have the power to make ourselves." – Swami Vivekananda

TAKE ACTION!

think positive

"I am the greatest, I said that even before I knew I was." – Muhammad Ali

NEVER EVER GIVE UP

think positive

"Take chances, make mistakes. That's how you grow. Pain nourishes your courage. You have to fail in order to practice being brave." – Mary Tyler Moore

MAKE IT HAPPEN

think positive

"If we're growing, we're always going to be out of our comfort zone." – John C Maxwell

BELIEVE YOU CAN

think positive

"The will to win, the desire to succeed, the urge to reach your full potential... these are the keys that will unlock the door to personal excellence." – Confucius

BELIEVE IN YOURSELF

think positive

"All you can change is yourself, but sometimes that changes everything!" – Gary W Goldstein

TAKE ACTION!

think positive

"Success is not a destination but the consciousness of knowing that you are enjoying what you are doing and by doing it every day you are rewarded with great results." - Frank Mullani

NEVER EVER GIVE UP

think positive

"No matter what the situation, remind yourself "I have a choice." – Deepak Chopra

MAKE IT HAPPEN

think positive

"If you think you can do a thing or think you can't do a thing, you're right." – Henry Ford

BELIEVE YOU CAN

think positive

"We are all here for some special reason. Stop being a prisoner of your past. Become the architect of your future." – Robin Sharma

BELIEVE IN YOURSELF

think positive

"Life is a gift, and it offers us the privilege, opportunity, and responsibility to give something back by becoming more." – Tony Robbins

TAKE ACTION!

think positive

"Today is a new beginning, a chance to turn your failures into achievements & your sorrows into so goods. No room for excuses."
— Joel Brown

NEVER EVER GIVE UP

think positive

"If you want light to come into your life, you need to stand where it is shining." – Guy Finley

MAKE IT
HAPPEN

think positive

"Happiness is an attitude. We either make ourselves miserable, or happy and strong. The amount of work is the same." – Francesca Reigler

BELIEVE YOU CAN

think positive

"Hope is a waking dream." – Aristotle

BELIEVE IN YOURSELF

think positive

"You yourself, as much as anybody in the entire universe, deserve your love and affection." – Buddha

TAKE ACTION!

think positive

"I've had a lot of worries in my life, most of which never happened" – Mark Twain

NEVER EVER GIVE UP

think positive

"Learning is a gift. Even when pain is your teacher." – Maya Watson

MAKE IT HAPPEN

think positive

"I may not have gone where I intended to go, but I think I have ended up where I needed to be." – Douglas Adams

BELIEVE YOU CAN

think positive

"Our greatest weakness lies in giving up. The most certain way to succeed is always to try just one more time." – Thomas Edison

BELIEVE IN YOURSELF

think positive

"We don't see things as they are, we see them as we are." – Anais Nin

TAKE ACTION!

think positive

"The only place where your dream becomes impossible is in your own thinking." – Robert H Schuller

NEVER EVER GIVE UP

think positive

"If you can dream it, then you can achieve it. You will get all you want in life if you help enough other people get what they want." – Zig Ziglar

MAKE IT HAPPEN

think positive

"Success consists of going from failure to failure without loss of enthusiasm." – Winston Churchill

BELIEVE YOU CAN

think positive

"An attitude of positive expectation is the mark of the superior personality." – Brian Tracy

BELIEVE IN YOURSELF

think positive

"If opportunity doesn't knock, build a door." – Milton Berle

TAKE ACTION!

think positive

"Believe in yourself! Have faith in your abilities! Without a humble but reasonable confidence in your own powers you cannot be successful or happy." – Norman Vincent Peale

NEVER EVER GIVE UP

think positive

"The way to get started is to quit talking and begin doing." - Walt Disney

MAKE IT HAPPEN

think positive

"Happiness is not something readymade. It comes from your own actions." - Dalai Lama

BELIEVE YOU CAN

think positive

"Challenges are what make life interesting and overcoming them is what makes life meaningful." - Joshua J. Marine

BELIEVE IN YOURSELF

think positive

"It is never too late to be what you might have been." - George Eliot

TAKE ACTION!

think positive

"Life is what we make it, always has been, always will be." - Grandma Moses

NEVER EVER GIVE UP

think positive

"I am thankful for all of those who said NO to me. Its because of them I'm doing it myself." - Albert Einstein

MAKE IT HAPPEN

think positive

"Do what makes YOU happy." - *Malcolm Matthews*

BELIEVE YOU CAN

think positive

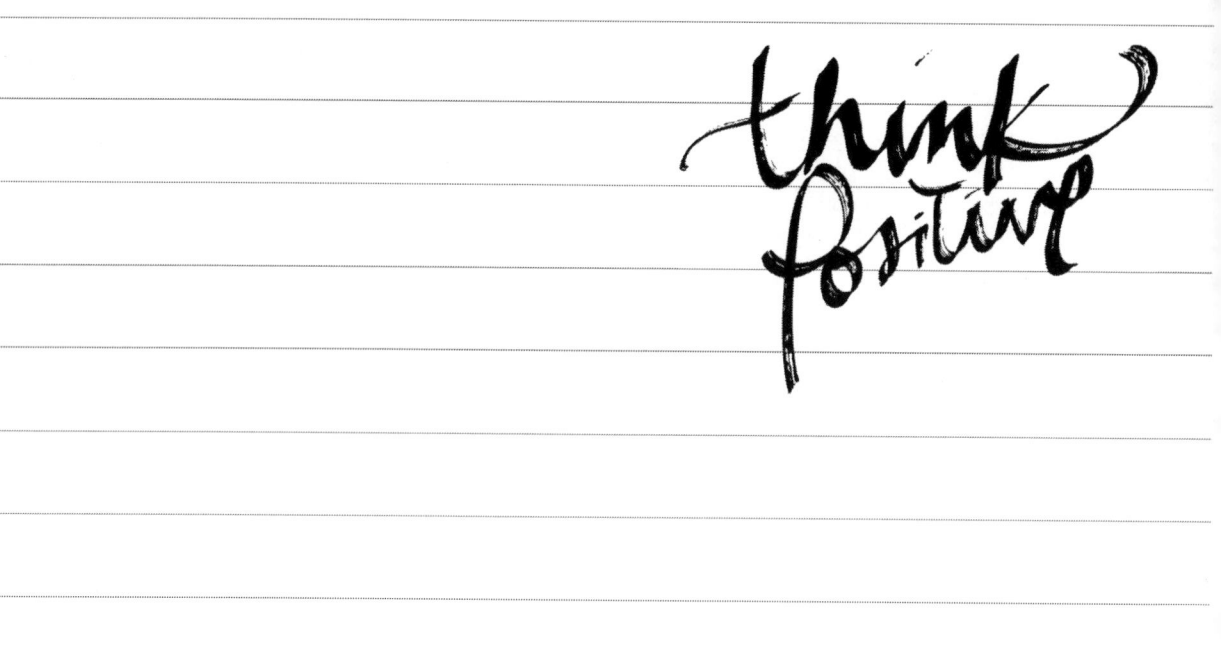

"The mind is everything. What you think you become." - Buddha

BELIEVE IN YOURSELF

BELIEVE IN YOURSELF

TAKE ACTION!

think positive

NEVER EVER GIVE UP

MAKE IT HAPPEN

THANK YOU WE HOPE YOU LIKE YOUR NOTEBOOK - JOURNAL
PLEASE WRITE YOUR REVIEW, IT MEANS A LOT TO US!

FIND MORE AMAZING JOURNALS, DIARIES & NOTEBOOKS AT:
www.CreativeJournalsFactory.com

Made in the USA
Lexington, KY
28 October 2018